CW00556338

MONTEVID TRAVEL GUIDE FOR BEGINNERS

The Updated Concise Guide for Planning a Trip to Montevideo Including Top Destinations,Culture,Outdoor Adventures,Cuisine and Getting Around

Nicolash Enzo

TABLE OF CONTENT

CHAPTER 1

INTRODUCTION

When strategizing a journey to the bustling metropolis of Montevideo, the capital of Uruguay, a primary and imperative factor to contemplate is the means of transportation to reach the destination. Located on the southern coast of South America, Montevideo has a range of transportation alternatives that provide visitors distinct experiences and perspectives of this captivating city. This comprehensive guide aims to provide travelers with essential information to facilitate a seamless and pleasurable trip, regardless of their mode of transportation, whether it air, land, or sea.

Air travel is a widely used kind of transportation, and one of the key components of this industry is airports. Carrasco International Airport is a prominent airport that plays a significant role in facilitating air travel.

The primary means of accessing Montevideo for a significant number of global passengers is by air transportation, with Carrasco International Airport (Aeropuerto Internacional de Carrasco) acting as the principal entry point for the city. The airport, situated around 13 miles (21 kilometers) east of the city center, derives its name after the renowned Uruguayan aviator. Carrasco, being the biggest and most heavily trafficked airport in Uruguay, has an array of amenities and provisions to accommodate the needs of both local and international passengers.

The airport's contemporary architectural features, distinguished by its undulating form, promptly provide an ambiance conducive to a distinctive travel experience. There are a considerable number of airlines that provide air transportation services to and from Carrasco, facilitating connections between Montevideo and prominent locations throughout the globe. The majority of international flights mostly originate from various locations in South America, North America, Europe, and other regions within the Southern Hemisphere.

Upon their arrival, guests have convenient access to the city core via a variety of transportation options. Taxis and ride-sharing services are easily accessible, providing a quick and pleasant means of transportation to reach one's lodging. Public transportation, such as buses, provide an economical option for anyone seeking to immerse themselves in the local mode of transportation.

Land Transportation: Buses, Trains, and Highways In the realm of land transportation, many modes of travel have emerged as prominent means of commuting. Buses, trains, and roads have become integral components of the transportation infrastructure, facilitating the movement of people and goods across vast

Although air travel is often considered the most expedient means of reaching Montevideo, traveling by road offers the unique chance to admire the picturesque scenery and immerse oneself in the local towns on route to the city.

The topic of discussion is buses. Uruguay has a comprehensive infrastructure of intercity buses, facilitating connectivity between Montevideo and several urban and rural areas around the nation. The Tres Cruces Terminal in Montevideo functions as a prominent transportation hub for buses, facilitating travel to many locations within Uruguay as well as neighboring countries such as Argentina and Brazil. The use of bus transportation provides individuals with the opportunity to see the rural landscape and immerse themselves in the authentic local culture.

The topic of discussion is trains. Although the railway network in Uruguay is relatively limited in comparison to other forms of transportation, there are train services that facilitate connections between Montevideo and neighboring municipalities such as Progreso and Las Piedras. The train travels provide a unique opportunity to explore the periphery of Montevideo and get a deeper understanding of the everyday routines and experiences of the local population.

In this section, we will discuss the topic of roads. When doing a road journey across South America, Montevideo may be conveniently reached via the use of well maintained roads and highways. Travelers have the opportunity to traverse the border from the adjacent countries of Argentina or Brazil, so benefiting from the freedom to halt at diverse areas of interest during their journey.

Sea travel is a popular kind of transportation for both leisure and commercial purposes. It encompasses two main types of vessels: cruise ships and ferries. These vessels serve as important transportation hubs, known as cruise ports and ferry terminals, facilitating the movement of passengers and goods across different destinations.

Montevideo has several opportunities for those who have a penchant for maritime transportation, since it gives the possibility of reaching the city by cruise or ferry, therefore affording a unique vantage point of its picturesque coastline.

One topic of interest in the field of tourism is cruise ports. Montevideo has become as a highly sought-after destination for cruise ships, as shown by the Port of Montevideo's recurrent inclusion in cruise itineraries. The act of arriving by cruise provides a unique opportunity to acquaint oneself with the city, as one is presented with a captivating view of its scenic cityscape from the water. Cruise guests are afforded the chance to engage with the many sights and cultural offerings of Montevideo, although within a constrained temporal context.

2. Ferries: The geographical closeness of Montevideo to Buenos Aires, Argentina, enables convenient transportation between

the two cities through ferry services. Ferry services are available for transportation over the Río de la Plata, providing a picturesque voyage lasting around two to three hours. This means of transportation not only offers convenience but also provides tourists with the opportunity to appreciate breathtaking vistas of the coastal region.

In summary, the process of reaching Montevideo offers a diverse range of options that accommodate various interests and travel approaches. Montevideo extends a warm welcome to travelers who possess a preference for the expeditiousness and ease of air transportation, the immersing nature of terrestrial expeditions, or the distinctive vantage point offered by sea voyages. Every method of transportation contributes a unique element of excitement to your journey, guaranteeing that your arrival in this intriguing metropolis marks only the start of an indelible encounter.

CHAPTER 2

Getting to Montevideo

Imagine a metropolis where the allure of colonial aesthetics converges with contemporary dynamism, where an abundance of cultural riches can be found, and where the essence of South America resonates throughout every nook and cranny. Montevideo, the alluring capital of Uruguay, entices visitors from across the world to go on a journey of discovery via its many attractions. However, prior to immersing oneself in the intricate cultural fabric and lively thoroughfares, the voyage itself assumes a crucial role in shaping the whole encounter. This thorough book explores the several pathways that take individuals to Montevideo, each presenting a unique opportunity for exploration, enabling travelers to embark on their journey well before arriving in this captivating city.

Air travel is a widely used kind of transportation, with airports serving as crucial hubs for facilitating the movement of passengers and goods. One such airport is Carrasco International Airport, which plays a significant role in the aviation industry.

For those traveling from faraway locations, the prevailing and expedient option for air transportation is Carrasco International Airport. The airport, which bears the name of the renowned Uruguayan pilot, serves as a symbol of contemporary design and operational effectiveness, evident in its streamlined architectural features and highly functional amenities. Located at a distance of around 13 miles (21 kilometers) east of the city center, this location serves as the main access point to Montevideo. Carrasco Airport facilitates the transportation of both internal and international planes, hence facilitating convenient connections from several global locations.

Upon disembarking from the aircraft, visitors are greeted by the warm reception of Uruguayan hospitality. The airport's architectural style, distinguished by its smooth contours and spacious interiors, provides a suitable introduction to a city that harmoniously combines elements of both heritage and contemporary. Numerous airlines, ranging from multinational carriers to regional operators, converge at one location, establishing worldwide links with cities across continents. The occurrence of this confluence guarantees that Montevideo's foreign tourists are presented with a wide array of choices to choose from.

After the aircraft lands, travelers may continue with their tour by exploring the diverse range of transportation alternatives that are accessible for commuting to the central area of Montevideo. Taxis and ride-sharing services are easily available, offering a convenient and efficient means of transportation to one's desired destination inside the urban area. If one wants to engage in the local culture and experience the rhythm of the city, using public buses may be a financially efficient method of seeing Montevideo. This mode of transportation offers the opportunity to catch glimpses of everyday life along the journey.

Land Transportation: Buses, Trains, and Roadways

Traveling to Montevideo through ground transportation provides an opportunity for a more immersive experience. The road and transport network of Uruguay, which is well interconnected, is an enticing invitation for passengers to go on journeys across its many landscapes and settlements on route to the capital.

One kind of transportation that is often used in urban areas is buses. The aesthetic allure of Uruguay becomes evident once one embarks on extensive bus voyages. The Tres Cruces Terminal in Montevideo functions as the central hub of an extensive transportation network, facilitating travel to many cities and villages around the country. The use of bus transportation facilitates a more profound level of interaction with the encompassing rural landscape, whereby expansive fields and charming villages provide fleeting insights into genuine Uruguayan culture.

The topic of discussion is trains. Although trains are not as widely used in Uruguay's transportation network compared to buses, they possess a unique and appealing quality. Montevideo maintains ties with neighboring towns, such as Progreso and Las Piedras. The train journeys, while with some limitations, provide a chance to interact with the local inhabitants while traversing the scenic landscapes.

In this section, we will discuss the topic of roads. For the adventurous explorer, undertaking a journey to Montevideo by road presents a captivating prospect. The presence of well-maintained roads and highways enables seamless travel between adjacent countries such as Argentina and Brazil, providing individuals with the opportunity to plan their itinerary and carefully choose their experiences during their journey. The expedition serves as a medium for creating indelible recollections.

Sea travel is a popular mode of transportation for both leisure and commercial purposes. It encompasses several means of maritime transportation, including cruise ports and ferries. These modes of sea travel serve as important gateways for passengers and cargo, facilitating connectivity between different regions and promoting tourism and trade. Cruise ports

The appeal of maritime transportation adds a sense of romanticism to one's voyage, providing distinctive views of the coastline of Montevideo.

One topic of interest in the field of tourism is cruise ports. Montevideo is well recognized as a very desirable port of call for cruise ships. The Port of Montevideo often appears on cruise itineraries, offering tourists the opportunity to disembark and engage with the city's cultural and historical attractions. The experience of arriving in the city by a cruise ship provides a unique and exceptional introduction, as the gradual emergence of the city's skyline against the water creates an incomparable visual spectacle. Although the amount of time available may be restricted, guests on a cruise have the opportunity to see significant landmarks, so obtaining a brief insight into the captivating charm of Montevideo.

Montevideo benefits from its geographical closeness to Buenos Aires, Argentina, since it enables convenient transportation between the two cities through ferry services. Traversing the Río de la Plata, a waterway that links the two cities, offers a unique route to Montevideo. The boat journey, lasting around two to three hours, offers a combination of ease and picturesque landscapes. Observing the coastal region from a maritime vantage point offers a novel outlook, intensifying the sense of expectation for the next expedition.

In summary, the expedition to Montevideo might be likened to a symphony, where each decision made has its own unique resonance. The choice of transportation method assumes a significant role in shaping the story, hence making a lasting impact on the anecdotes one shares after the exploration of Montevideo's streets. Regardless of the mode of transportation, the chosen route guarantees that the commencement of your voyage occurs well in advance of your arrival in this enchanting urban center. Therefore, it is recommended that individuals fully embrace the experience, relish each moment, and allow the voyage to imbue their recollections of Montevideo with a profound feeling of exploration that is just as rewarding as the ultimate goal.

CHAPTER 3

Exploring the City of Montevideo

Located on the picturesque beaches of the Río de la Plata, Montevideo, the bustling capital of Uruguay, eagerly anticipates your discovery. Montevideo, a city characterized by the coexistence of colonial architecture and contemporary constructions, resonates with historical echoes that permeate its cobblestone streets. Moreover, the strong cultural vitality that pervades every part of the city entices visitors with a diverse array of experiences, creating a tapestry of opportunities waiting to be explored. This thorough guide aims to provide an in-depth exploration of Montevideo's districts, sites, museums, and gastronomic offerings, revealing the many elements that contribute to the city's allure as a compelling destination.

Ciudad Vieja, also known as the Old City, has a significant place in historical narratives.

Ciudad Vieja, the ancient Old Town of Montevideo, serves as a significant portal to the past, showcasing the enduring colonial legacy of the city. One may meander through the small alleyways, where architectural marvels serve as tangible testaments to the progression of time. The focal point of Ciudad Vieja is the renowned Plaza Independencia, a plaza that harmoniously combines historical and contemporary elements. The sombre tomb of José Artigas, Uruguay's national hero, presents a striking juxtaposition to the vibrant commercial activity and towering architectural structures that surround its vicinity.

The Solís Theatre is a prominent cultural institution in Uruguay. The Solís Theatre, a neoclassical masterpiece, has been an esteemed addition to the architectural landscape of Ciudad Vieja in Montevideo since its establishment in 1856. The sumptuous interiors and elaborate façade of the structure stand as a tribute to the cultural sophistication of the city. The act of attending a performance at this esteemed theater provides an opportunity to get insight into Montevideo's rich creative legacy, therefore highlighting the city's profound admiration for opera, ballet, and theater.

The Rambla of Montevideo is a picturesque coastal promenade that offers a serene and tranquil atmosphere.

The Rambla of Montevideo, spanning a distance of more than 13 miles (21 kilometers) along the coastline, represents a picturesque promenade that encapsulates the fundamental connection between the city and the sea. At the onset of dusk, those residing in the area as well as tourists congregate to engage in leisurely activities such as walking, jogging, cycling, or just appreciating the serene atmosphere. The vast promenade is adorned with public green spaces, coastal stretches, and facilities for leisure activities, creating an enticing atmosphere that encourages relaxation and fosters a connection with the natural ebb and flow of the sea.

Pocitos and Punta Carretas: An Analysis of Urban Charisma

Pocitos, a district in Montevideo, is well recognized for its contemporary appeal, emanating an urban charm that captivates both residents and tourists alike. The city's expansive boulevards are adorned with a plethora of upscale shops, charming cafes, and exquisite dining establishments, resulting in an ambiance that seamlessly blends refinement with tranquility. Pocitos Beach is a highly frequented destination among those seeking recreational activities by the seaside, owing to its appealing sandy shores and tranquil undulations of water.

Punta Carretas, situated in close proximity to Pocitos, is a neighborhood that effectively amalgamates historical elements with contemporary features. The Punta Carretas Lighthouse, which has served as a navigational aid since 1876, is situated in close proximity to the Punta Carretas Shopping Mall. This mall, known for its contemporary shop offerings, is located inside a refurbished penitentiary. This makeover exemplifies Montevideo's capacity to commemorate its historical heritage while also embracing the prospects of the future.

Parque Rodó and Parque Batlle: Urban Green Spaces

Montevideo's abundant verdant areas, particularly Parque Rodó and Parque Batlle, serve as havens for those who possess a deep appreciation for the natural world. Parque Rodó is an expansive sanctuary that provides respite from the bustling metropolitan environment. The tranquil lakes, artistic sculptures, and meandering walkways of this location provide an ideal setting for leisurely walks or outdoor dining experiences. The National Museum of Visual Arts is located inside this park, providing an opportunity to delve into Uruguay's creative legacy among the surrounding natural splendor.

In contrast, Parque Batlle is the location of the renowned Estadio Centenario, a site of great significance for football aficionados due to its role as the host venue for the first FIFA World Cup in 1930. This expansive park serves as a tribute to physical activities and leisure pursuits, attracting community members who engage in activities such as running, cycling, and even partaking in picnics. The enormous green space of the park offers a peek of Montevideo's dedication to promoting a healthy lifestyle and engaging in outdoor activities.

Museums and cultural sites play a crucial role in fostering and nurturing creativity.

The cultural environment of Montevideo is enhanced by a diverse selection of museums and places that commemorate its historical, artistic, and traditional aspects.

The National Museum of Visual Arts is an institution dedicated to the exhibition and preservation of visual artworks. Situated inside the confines of Parque Rodó, the museum in question serves as a repository for a vast assemblage of artistic creations originating from Uruguay and many other parts of the world. The collection encompasses a wide temporal range, commencing with the 19th century and extending to modern artistic endeavors. The galleries of this establishment exhibit a remarkable assortment of paintings, sculptures, and decorative arts, providing valuable perspectives on the aesthetic development of Uruguay.

The Museo Torres García is a renowned cultural institution that showcases the artistic works of Joaquín Torres García. The museum in question pays homage to the life and artistic contributions of the renowned artist Joaquín Torres García, who is well respected in the field. The museum's collection and displays provide an insightful perspective into the significant impact of Torres García on the development of contemporary art in Uruguay and its broader effect.

The Museo Nacional de Artes Visuales is a prominent institution dedicated to the exhibition and preservation of visual arts. Located inside the premises of a former palace, the museum in question serves as an abundant repository of visual art. The collection encompasses a diverse range of genres, ranging from traditional to modern, so exemplifying the varied and eclectic aspect of Uruguay's art scene.

The Museo Carnaval is a cultural institution that showcases the history and traditions of carnival celebrations. Explore the rich carnival culture of Uruguay at this museum, dedicated to commemorating the nation's foremost yearly celebration. The use of costumes, masks, and displays serves as a means to exhibit the historical and cultural essence of carnival, so offering visitors an immersive encounter with this extravagant cultural phenomenon.

Exploring Culinary Delights: An Exploration of Uruguay's Distinctive Flavors

One cannot consider their study of Montevideo to be complete without partaking in its many gastronomic offers. The culinary traditions of Uruguay are a manifestation of its rich cultural legacy and agricultural expertise.

The term asado refers to a traditional South American barbecue cooking technique. The asado, a fundamental element of Uruguayan culture, is a longstanding barbecue custom whereby several meat slices are cooked over an exposed flame. The act of engaging in this gastronomic tradition is often savored in the company of companions and loved ones, embodying the fundamental principles of collective meal sharing.

The term Chivito refers to a traditional dish originating from Uruguay. The chivito, a renowned sandwich originating from Uruguay, consists of succulent sirloin complemented with ham, cheese, lettuce, tomato, and many condiments. This dish exemplifies Uruguay's commitment to culinary enjoyment, offering a rich and tasty experience.

Empanadas are a type of pastry that originated in Spain and are popular in many Latin These delectable pastries are a ubiquitous street dish, providing a convenient and palatable morsel. Empanadas, which are often consumed in Uruguay, are savory pastries that encapsulate a variety of fillings such as meat, cheese, or vegetables. These delectable treats are renowned for their portability and ability to capture the distinct tastes of Uruguayan cuisine.

The Mercado del Puerto is a renowned marketplace located in Montevideo, Uruguay. Mercado del Puerto, a renowned gastronomic destination, is a vibrant market permeated by the enticing scent of grilled meats. In this locale, one may indulge in regional delicacies, with a particular emphasis on the esteemed Uruguayan beef, expertly crafted by proficient grillmasters.

The presence of local cafés and restaurants in a given area is a notable aspect of its culinary landscape. These establishments serve as gathering places for those seeking a variety of food and beverage options. The eating landscape of Montevideo has a wide range of culinary establishments. A wide range of culinary establishments, including both classic parrillas (steakhouses) and modern fusion restaurants, can be found, offering a diverse selection of gastronomic delights to satisfy all tastes and preferences.

Title: The Allure of Nightlife and Entertainment: A Study in Nocturnal Enchantment The subject of this study is on the captivating aspects of nightlife and entertainment, particularly during the nighttime hours.

As the sun descends below the horizon in Montevideo, the urban environment undergoes a transformation, giving rise to a vibrant nocturnal culture that offers a wide range of entertainment alternatives.

Bars and pubs are establishments that provide alcoholic beverages for use on-site. These establishments often provide a social environment for individuals to gather and socialize while enjoying alcoholic beverages. Montevideo's bar culture has a wide range of establishments, from historically significant bars exuding a timeless elegance to contemporary pubs with a modern flare. This diversity is reflective of the city's many districts. Indulge in the consumption of regional artisanal beers, traditional mixed drinks, and the conviviality of like-minded individuals.

The topic of discussion pertains to clubs and music venues. Montevideo's clubs and music venues provide a vibrant ambiance for anyone desiring to engage in nocturnal dancing activities. Individuals with diverse musical inclinations might discover a suitable place according to their interests, whether it electronic beats, Latin rhythms, or live bands.

Cultural

The topic of discussion pertains to performances. The cultural calendar of Montevideo is replete with a diverse array of activities, including theatrical shows as well as live music concerts. To get exposure to the vibrant creative scene of the city, it is advisable to consult local listings in order to attend intriguing performances.

Day Trips and Nearby Attractions: Broadening Perspectives

While Montevideo itself provides a plethora of activities, the encompassing area beckons for adventure outside the confines of the city.

This particular colonial village, designated as a UNESCO World Heritage Site, is conveniently accessible through a short boat journey from Montevideo. This location offers a charming ambiance characterized by cobblestone alleys, well-preserved medieval houses, and a picturesque riverfront environment, all of which combine to create an enticing destination for visitors.

Punta del Este is a renowned coastal city located in southeastern Uruguay. Punta del Este, a seaside resort town situated a few hours away from Montevideo, is sometimes likened to the renowned St. Tropez of South America. The location is characterized by its unspoiled coastlines, high-end retail establishments, artistic exhibition spaces, and a lively after-dark entertainment scene.

The topic of discussion is to the many geographical areas that are known for their production of wine. Uruguay's emerging wine areas are located within a day's travel from Montevideo. Canelones and Maldonado regions have a plethora of vineyards and wineries that beckon visitors to partake in the experience of tastings and guided excursions. The renowned wine variety of Tannat, which is emblematic of Uruguay, is eagerly poised to be savored by those with refined taste.

Engaging in Outdoor Activities: Embracing the Natural Environment

Montevideo and its environs provide a wide array of opportunities for those who like engaging in outdoor activities, allowing them to establish a profound connection with the natural environment.

Water sports refer to recreational activities that take place in or on water bodies, such as lakes, rivers, or oceans. These activities The coastline of Montevideo is an enticing opportunity for water enthusiasts to partake in a variety of sports, including surfing, sailing, kayaking, and windsurfing. Both local schools and rental facilities provide services for individuals at all skill levels, including beginners and specialists.

The topic of discussion pertains to cycling and walking tours. Explore the urban environment at your preferred speed by engaging in bike or walking excursions. These immersive experiences provide individuals the opportunity to investigate the many neighborhoods, monuments, and hidden treasures of Montevideo.

Hiking is a recreational activity that involves walking in natural environments, typically on trails or paths Although the city of Montevideo is mostly characterized by its flat topography, there are adjacent natural regions that provide trekking options for anyone who like to explore the surrounding hills and enjoy the scenic vistas of the region.

Exploring Montevideo's Shopping Scene: Discovering Valuable Artifacts and Souvenirs

The possibility of acquiring a memento from Montevideo is rather pleasurable, owing to the presence of several retail areas and marketplaces inside the city.

The topic of discussion pertains to distinctive souvenirs. Investigate several marketplaces and shops that provide a wide range of locally produced crafts, leather items, and artisanal products. Memorable keepsakes may be obtained via the acquisition of handcrafted handicrafts and distinctly Uruguayan presents.

The topic of discussion pertains to shopping districts. Explore several areas such as Pocitos and Ciudad Vieja, which are characterized by the presence of boutique boutiques, galleries, and concept shops that showcase a diverse selection of well picked items.

The topic of discussion pertains to antiques and collectibles. Montevideo's antiques stores and marketplaces provide an enticing opportunity for anyone with a penchant for vintage artifacts to discover distinctive and enduring pieces.

Practical Recommendations for Travelers: Facilitating Navigation

Prior to commencing your journey in Montevideo, it is advisable to take into account certain practical factors that will contribute to an enhanced travel experience.

The topic of safety is of utmost importance and warrants careful consideration. Montevideo is often regarded as a secure destination for vacationers. Nevertheless, similar to any urban area, it is recommended to use care and adhere to fundamental safety measures.

The topic of discussion is currency exchange. The designated monetary unit of Uruguay is the Uruguayan peso (UYU). Currency exchange services may be found in financial institutions such as banks, dedicated exchange offices, and select hotels.

The user's text is already academic in nature. No rewriting is necessary. Uruguay designates Spanish as its official language. In the tourist sector, possessing a rudimentary understanding of Spanish words might be advantageous in facilitating improved communication, despite the prevalence of English speakers.

Etiquette in the Local Context: Uruguayans are renowned for their amiable disposition and welcoming nature. In many cultures, it is common to initiate social interactions by engaging in a handshake or exchanging a kiss on the cheek. Gratuities are often expected and valued in the context of dining establishments and in exchange for provided services.

As our investigation of Montevideo nears its conclusion, we come to the understanding that this urban center is more than just a place to visit; it is a complex composition interlaced with historical events, cultural expressions, and the ambitions of its inhabitants. The city of Montevideo extends an invitation to individuals to explore its urban landscape and engage in a comprehensive cultural experience, ranging from the impressive architectural structures found in the historic district of Ciudad Vieja to the serene ambiance of the Rambla. The museums, marketplaces, and gastronomic offerings of a country provide valuable insights into its cultural essence, while its breathtaking natural landscapes and proximity to other attractions beckon individuals to explore beyond its borders.

Montevideo entices tourists not just to watch, but also to actively participate in its narrative, to interact with its liveliness, and to embrace the dynamic balance between tradition and modernity that characterizes its fundamental nature. Montevideo, the capital city of Uruguay, offers a multitude of experiences that make a lasting impression on visitors. From indulging in the delectable flavors of a chivito, a traditional Uruguayan dish, to immersing oneself in the historical significance of its cobblestone streets, or being captivated by the vibrant energy of its nightlife,

Montevideo's allure lingers in one's memory even after departing from its embrace. One is encouraged to immerse oneself in the allure of Montevideo, allowing the senses to serve as a compass, as this city leaves an indelible mark on one's recollections, beckoning with its inviting charm, enchanting with its many pleasures, and captivating at every juncture.

CHAPTER 4

Culinary Experiences

Food, in addition to its inherent nutritional properties, serves as a conduit for the exploration and understanding of many cultural, historical, and identity-related aspects. In the city of Montevideo, which serves as the capital of Uruguay, one may see a series of gastronomic encounters that resemble the progression of chapters inside a riveting narrative. Each dish presented can be likened to a page, unveiling the profound cultural legacy of the country and the lively essence of the urban landscape. Montevideo's culinary landscape encompasses a diverse range of gastronomic offerings, spanning from classic and robust dishes to contemporary and inventive creations.

This vibrant culinary scene entices visitors to embark on a delightful exploration, one that not only gratifies the senses but also nurtures the spirit and cultivates a profound bond with the city and its inhabitants.

Uruguayan cuisine: A fusion of many flavors

Uruguayan cuisine exemplifies the amalgamation of numerous cultural elements that have been interwoven over the course of centuries, resulting in the development of a distinctive gourmet fabric. The fusion of Indigenous customs, European heritage, and African influences results in the creation of culinary offerings that exhibit a balanced blend of familiarity and distinctiveness.

Asado: The Pulsating Core of Uruguayan Gastronomy

The fundamental essence of Uruguayan gastronomic culture is centered on the esteemed practice of asado, an immersive barbeque encounter that surpasses ordinary sustenance and evolves into a ceremonial expression of communal unity. The asado is more than a mere culinary experience; rather, it embodies a commemoration of communal bonds, familial ties, and the mastery of the grilling craft.

Imagine a scenario where luscious portions of meat are meticulously seasoned and cooked slowly over an exposed fire, yielding a delectable outcome characterized by a smokey, tender, and flavorsome profile. In the city of Montevideo, the culinary tradition of asado has significant cultural importance and is deeply ingrained in the daily lives of its inhabitants. A wide range of culinary preparations may be seen in the use of various parts of the animal, such as beef ribs, sausages, sweetbreads, and blood sausages, resulting in delectable and very appealing gastronomic creations. The olfactory perception of the aroma emitted by cooking meat permeates the atmosphere, coinciding with the occurrence of social events taking place in residential outdoor spaces, specialized establishments dedicated to the preparation of grilled meat, and even public thoroughfares. Both residents and tourists gather to engage in this cherished gastronomic tradition, where they together exchange laughs, anecdotes, and the sheer delight of participating in such an activity.

The Chivito: An Emblem of Robustness

The chivito is regarded as a culinary symbol that should not be overlooked by anyone in search of a substantial and gratifying dinner. The chivito, a sandwich that has gained popularity in Uruguayan cuisine, derives its name from the diminutive version of the Spanish word chivo, meaning goat. The central component of this dish consists of a delicate cut of beef, often accompanied by layers of cured pork, cheese, leafy greens, ripe tomato, and a fried ovum. The chivito, a culinary creation that showcases Uruguay's affinity for meat and comfort cuisine, is presented alongside a diverse assortment of sauces and accompanied by a delectable serving of crispy fries. This harmonious combination of tastes results in a culinary experience that is both satisfying and representative of the country's culinary traditions.

Empanadas: A Convenient Culinary Pleasure

Empanadas, a widely consumed delicacy across Latin America, have a significant role within the culinary heritage of Uruguay. These delectable pastries, often savored as popular street food or appetizers, exhibit a lovely amalgamation of diverse tastes and contrasting textures. The dough is often filled with a diverse range of ingredients, including meat, cheese, veggies, and spices. Empanadas, when baked to a state of golden perfection, provide a convenient and gratifying culinary experience that encapsulates the distinctive tastes of Uruguayan cuisine inside a portable format.

The Mercado del Puerto: A Paradise for Meat Lovers

For those who are enthusiastic about immersing themselves in Montevideo's gastronomic landscape, Mercado del Puerto presents itself as a haven of diverse tastes and fragrances. The vibrant marketplace serves as a sanctuary for those who consume meat, as proficient grillmasters exhibit their expertise and provide a captivating display of culinary prowess. Mercado del Puerto offers a remarkable chance to see the culinary spectacle of asado, showcasing succulent meat cuts and sizzling sausages on the grill. Within the captivating ambiance and alluring aromas, individuals have the opportunity to partake in an asado banquet that satiates not only their hunger but also piques their interest in the culinary customs of Uruguay.

Local cafés and restaurants: An amalgamation of traditional and contemporary elements

While Montevideo's culinary environment is characterized by the presence of classic cuisine, the city also demonstrates a receptiveness to innovation and current influences. The local establishments, namely cafés and restaurants, provide a wide array of choices that include a variety of global influences and incorporate locally sourced foods. This amalgamation of culinary elements aims to provide dining experiences that appeal to both the indigenous population and visitors alike.

The topic of discussion is fusion cuisine. The gastronomic landscape of Montevideo is characterized by a captivating amalgamation of tastes. In the realm of modern dining establishments, there is a prevalent practice of amalgamating conventional Uruguayan foodstuffs with global culinary methods and ideas, yielding gastronomic creations that evoke astonishment and gratification in the discerning taste buds. These inventive dishes exemplify the city's receptiveness to innovation while maintaining a strong connection to its culinary tradition.

The topic of discussion is Seafood Delights. Montevideo, because to its coastal geographical position, has a plethora of opportunities to indulge in the consumption of freshly caught seafood. The city's restaurants provide a diverse range of culinary options that highlight the abundance of marine tastes, ranging from grilled fish to seafood stews. Regional seafood such as sea bass, squid, and shrimp are included into culinary offerings, providing a pleasing juxtaposition to the mostly meat-based fare.

The topic of discussion pertains to wines produced within a certain geographical region. A comprehensive gastronomic investigation of Montevideo necessitates the inclusion of a taste of Uruguay's esteemed wines. The wine-producing areas of the nation, namely Canelones and Maldonado, are renowned for their diverse range of high-quality wines, with Tannat being well recognized as the signature grape variety. Enthusiasts of wine and those with less knowledge in the subject may both participate in wine tours and tastings, so acquiring valuable knowledge about Uruguay's wine production customs and the distinctive attributes of its terroir.

In this section, we will discuss the establishments known as cafés and bakeries. The café culture of Montevideo is characterized by a harmonious combination of leisure and social bonding. The act of enjoying a cortado, which is a combination of espresso and a tiny quantity of milk, at a café situated along a street, or indulging in a medialuna, a kind of croissant, at a nearby bakery, reveals that these establishments have a purpose beyond the mere provision of sustenance. They also foster social interaction and facilitate meaningful dialogue.

Practical Strategies for Food Enthusiasts: Navigating the Culinary Terrain

When embarking on a gastronomic exploration of Montevideo, it is advisable to consider a few practical considerations that might improve your overall experience.

Explore Regional Delicacies: Embrace the chance to indulge in authentic meals such as asado (barbecue) and chivito (a sandwich with grilled meat), as they provide valuable insights into the culinary heritage of Uruguay.

The operating hours of the dining facility are as follows: It is important to note that dinner hours in Montevideo may vary from those observed in other countries. Lunch is often had around the hours of 1:00 PM and

3:00 PM, whilst the commencement of supper typically occurs at 9:00 PM or later.

The topic of reservations is of significant academic interest. It is recommended to engage in the practice of making reservations, particularly during periods of high demand for dining services or at establishments that are highly sought after, in order to guarantee the acquisition of a table.

The topic of interest is the use of cash and cards as forms of payment. Although credit cards are often accepted, it is advisable to have cash on hand for smaller restaurants and street sellers.

The user's text is already academic in nature. No rewriting is necessary. Acquiring a rudimentary understanding of fundamental Spanish expressions might augment one's gastronomic encounter, since it is well acknowledged that local people value the endeavor to engage in conversation using their mother language.

In the city of Montevideo, culinary experiences transcend mere subsistence and serve as a gateway to understanding the essence and spirit of a country. Every culinary creation, regardless of its adherence to traditional practices or incorporation of innovative elements, has a narrative that intricately weaves together with the historical, cultural, and societal fabric of Uruguay. Montevideo's culinary options provide guests with an opportunity to intimately connect with the city's character via engaging in sensory and gastronomic experiences, ranging from the social delight of asado gatherings to the delectable tastes of chivito and empanadas.

While immersing oneself in Montevideo's parrillas, cafés, and marketplaces, it becomes evident that the gastronomic experience extends beyond just consumption. The experience transforms into a commemoration of existence, an act of fellowship with historical events, and an avenue for establishing relationships with community members who get satisfaction from imparting their culinary traditions. Allow your gustatory senses to serve as a navigational tool as you explore the streets of Montevideo, for each morsel consumed to serve as a stroke of a brush on the canvas of your recollections of travel, thereby forming a vibrant tapestry of tastes that will forever be interwoven with your encounter with this enchanting urban center.

CHAPTER 5

Outdoor Activities

Montevideo, the dynamic capital of Uruguay, serves as both a thriving metropolitan center and a portal to a realm of natural marvels and outdoor exploits. In addition to the urban environment and notable points of interest, there exists a vast array of awe-inspiring natural landscapes, varied ecosystems, and stimulating recreational pursuits that entice people to go outside the confines of the city and fully immerse themselves in the splendor of the natural world. Montevideo and its environs have a diverse range of outdoor activities, including pleasant seaside getaways, exhilarating water sports, peaceful parks, and challenging hikes, all of which appeal to the adventurous inclinations of individuals. In this book, we extend an invitation to accompany us on a trip as we delve into the abundant array of outdoor activities that lie in wait within the vicinity of Montevideo.

The Rambla of Montevideo is a serene coastal promenade that offers a peaceful and tranquil experience to visitors.

The Rambla of Montevideo extends along the city's shoreline, resembling a serene strip that offers an urban retreat for both residents and tourists, allowing them to appreciate the scenic charm of the Río de la Plata. The extensive promenade provides an ideal environment for leisurely walks, energetic jogs, and tranquil reflection along the waterfront.

Throughout the day, the Rambla presents dynamic and evolving views that reflect the temporal progression from dawn to dusk. The dawn illuminates the atmosphere with gentle shades, beckoning those engaged in jogging and cycling to embrace the beginning of the day with vitality. Throughout the course of the day, the Rambla attracts many individuals, including families, couples, and friends, who are in search of a temporary escape from the fast-paced nature of metropolitan life. The evening sunsets emit a radiant warmth onto the ocean, creating an ambiance of tranquility that attracts both individuals and groups to appreciate the uncomplicated delight of seeing the sun go below the horizon.

Water sports and beach adventures provide exciting opportunities for individuals to engage in thrilling activities. These activities provide a unique avenue for individuals to immerse themselves in exhilarating experiences and explore the wonders of the ocean.

Due to its coastal setting, Montevideo offers a diverse range of recreational opportunities for anyone with an affinity for water-related activities. The city's beaches provide a variety of water activities that accommodate a wide range of interests, including serene bays and dynamic rolling waves.

Playa Pocitos and Playa Brava are well recognized as prominent destinations for the sport of surfing. Montevideo's beaches provide an optimal environment for individuals of varying surfing expertise levels, ranging from experienced practitioners to novices seeking to experience the exhilaration of riding waves. Surf schools operating within the local area provide comprehensive instructional sessions and facilitate the rental of necessary equipment, so guaranteeing equitable access for anyone to engage in the activity of wave riding.

The topic of discussion pertains to the activities of sailing and boating. The tranquil expanse of the Río de la Plata offers an ideal setting for engaging in various nautical pursuits like as sailing, kayaking, and other forms of boating. Embark on a maritime journey and examine the coastal region from a novel vantage point, or engage in a leisurely paddling activity along the serene shoreline while immersing oneself in the surrounding pristine environment.

The present discourse aims to examine the sports of windsurfing and kiteboarding, exploring their respective characteristics, techniques, and equipment. Playa Malvín serves as a prominent destination for windsurfing and kiteboarding, drawing in those who possess a fervent passion for using the kinetic force of the wind to gracefully traverse the surface of the ocean. These beaches provide optimal circumstances for engaging in exciting water sports due to their consistent breezes and expansive bodies of water.

Cycling and walking tours provide opportunities for urban exploration.

Although Montevideo has a variety of outdoor attractions outside its municipal limits, the urban environment inside the city itself provides many opportunities for exploration. Cycling and walking excursions provide a more immersive approach to seeing the many districts, architectural wonders, and hidden gems inside the city.

The topic of discussion is cycling. Montevideo is characterized by its extensive network of bike-friendly pathways and lanes, which contribute to the pleasant experience of riding as a means of transportation and a means of exploring the city. One may choose to rent a bicycle and begin a voyage around the many neighborhoods of the city, therefore experiencing the visual, auditory, and communal aspects that manifest along the chosen path.

Walking tours are a popular kind of tourism that involves seeing a city or a specific area on foot. This type of tour allows participants Guided walking tours provide a comprehensive understanding of Montevideo's historical, cultural, and architectural aspects. Embark upon an enlightening journey through several districts such as Ciudad Vieja, Pocitos, and

Punta Carretas, accompanied by erudite guides who adeptly impart narratives and tales that vividly illuminate the historical and contemporary essence of the city.

Urban parks have emerged as important spaces that bring nature into the heart of the city.

The city of Montevideo has a strong dedication to the preservation of green areas within its urban environment, as seen by the meticulous upkeep of its parks and gardens. These natural oasis provide a pleasant break from the fast-paced metropolitan environment and an opportunity to reestablish a connection with the natural world.

Parque Rodó is a public park located in the city of Montevideo, Uruguay. It is named for the prominent Ur Located in the vicinity of Pocitos and Punta Carretas, Parque Rodó is a well regarded urban park that provides a tranquil respite from the bustling atmosphere of the city. The park's serene lakes, shaded walkways, and artistic sculptures provide an inviting atmosphere that encourages people to leisurely walk, have a picnic, and relax.

Parque Batlle is a public park located in the city of Montevideo, Uruguay. The vast park in question serves not only as a recreational sanctuary, but also as the site of the renowned Estadio Centenario, a significant football stadium that played host to the first FIFA World Cup in 1930. The grassy grounds of Parque Batlle provide as a scenic setting for activities such as picnicking, engaging in outdoor sports, and unwinding.

Exploring Natural Reserves and Hiking Trails: Venturing into the Untamed Wilderness

Montevideo's environs provide a plethora of possibilities for anyone desiring to fully engage with the natural world. These include the chance to participate in activities like as hiking, birding, and the exploration of several natural reserves.

The Santa Lucía Hill Natural Park is a notable location that warrants academic attention. Located in close proximity to Montevideo, this park serves as a sanctuary for those who like hiking and have a deep appreciation for the natural world. Embark on a trek to the peak of Cerro de la Victoria to see expansive vistas, traverse scenic footpaths, and encounter historical landmarks that enhance the richness of your outdoor sojourn.

Laguna del Sauce is a prominent geographical feature located in Uruguay. Situated beyond the urban area, the Laguna del Sauce is a tranquil body of water surrounded by verdant scenery. The region is home to a wide variety of bird species, which will undoubtedly provide great joy to birdwatching enthusiasts. Individuals with a penchant for outdoor activities have the opportunity to engage in invigorating pursuits such as hiking, kayaking, or immersing themselves in the serene ambiance of this pristine natural sanctuary.

The Pajas Blancas Dam is a significant infrastructure project that has been constructed in a particular region. The reservoir has hiking paths that lead to vantage spots offering panoramic views of the massive dam. The pathways meander across undulating terrain, providing an opportunity for anyone to establish a connection with the natural environment and appreciate awe-inspiring vistas.

Practical Strategies for Outdoor Excursions: Preparatory Measures and Pleasurable Experiences

When engaging in outdoor activities in and around Montevideo, it is advisable to bear in mind the following practical recommendations in order to guarantee a secure and pleasurable experience:

The topic of sun protection is of utmost importance when considering the potential harm caused by exposure to the sun's rays. The solar radiation in Uruguay may be quite strong, particularly in the summer season. In order to safeguard oneself from the harmful effects of solar radiation, it is advisable to use protective measures such as applying sunscreen, donning a hat, and wearing sunglasses.

The topic of discussion is hydration. It is essential to maintain proper hydration, particularly while participating in outdoor activities. It is advisable to bring a water bottle and schedule periodic intervals for hydration.

Suitable Attire Selection: Opt for attire that is both comfortable and appropriate for the specific activity you will be participating in.

It is vital to own the suitable equipment for engaging in water activities.

Compliance with Local legislation: It is important to adhere to and abide by the local legislation and norms while participating in outdoor activities. Certain regions may implement unique regulations in order to protect the environment and maintain the well-being of people.

The topic of wildlife awareness is of utmost importance in the field of environmental studies. When engaging in the exploration of natural environments, it is important to exercise caution and consideration towards the many forms of animals and their respective ecosystems. It is advisable to maintain a safe distance from animals and refrain from causing any disturbances.

Factors to Consider Regarding Weather Conditions: It is advisable to consult the weather forecast before to embarking on any outside activities. It is advisable to anticipate fluctuations in meteorological conditions and make appropriate modifications to your itinerary.

The fascination of Montevideo transcends its metropolitan beauty, as it entices those with a spirit of adventure to delve into the wonders of the natural world, immersing themselves in a diverse array of landscapes that include both tranquil coastal areas and challenging rocky routes. The outdoor activities available in and around Montevideo provide individuals with the opportunity to appreciate and engage with the natural environment. Whether it is sailing on a sailboat, seeing lesser-known attractions on a bicycle trip, or just enjoying the peacefulness of a park, these activities allow individuals to immerse themselves in the splendor, liveliness, and awe-inspiring aspects of nature.

Each action offers an opportunity to disengage from the digital realm and reestablish a connection with the natural world's inherent rhythms. When engaging in hiking, water sports, and urban explorations in Montevideo, one will come to realize that the city's outdoor activities serve a purpose beyond mere recreation. They present individuals with the chance to revitalize themselves, seek comfort, and forge lasting memories imbued with the vibrant colors of sunsets, the gentle murmurs of waves, and the splendor of expansive skies. Therefore, it is advisable to respond to the innate want to engage with the natural environment, travel outside, and use the captivating aesthetics of Montevideo's landscapes to serve as a wellspring of motivation, exploration, and harmonious interaction with the surrounding world.

THE END

Printed in Great Britain
by Amazon